PRIMARY SOURCES IN AMERICAN HISTORY

WOMEN'S SUFFRAGE
A PRIMARY SOURCE HISTORY OF THE WOMEN'S RIGHTS MOVEMENT IN AMERICA

COLLEEN ADAMS

rosen central
Primary Source

*To my mom, who always has the determination and courage
to live her life as a truly independent woman*

Published in 2003 by The Rosen Publishing Group, Inc.
29 East 21st Street, New York, NY 10010

First Edition

Library of Congress Cataloging-in-Publication Data

Adams, Colleen, 1955–
Women's suffrage: a primary source history of the women's rights
movement in America / Colleen Adams.— 1st ed.
   p. cm. — (Primary sources in American history)
Includes bibliographical references and index.
ISBN 0-8239-3685-6 (lib. bdg.)
1. Women's rights—United States—History—Juvenile literature. 2. Women's
rights—United States—History—Sources. 3. Women—Suffrage—United
States—History—Juvenile literature. 4. Women—Suffrage—United States—
History—Sources. I. Title. II. Series.

HQ1236.5.U6 O34 2003
305.42'0973—dc21

                                                            2002004476

Manufactured in the United States of America

CONTENTS

Introduction Early Supporters of Women's Rights • **4**

Timeline • **7**

Chapter 1 Women's Influence on Early
Social Reform Movements • **12**

Chapter 2 Leaders of the Women's Rights
Movement in the 1850s • **20**

Chapter 3 Elizabeth Cady Stanton Makes a Difference • **24**

Chapter 4 Susan B. Anthony and the
Fight for Women's Suffrage • **32**

Chapter 5 The Struggle for the Vote Continues • **37**

Primary Source Transcriptions • **51**

Glossary • **56**

For More Information • **59**

For Further Reading • **59**

Bibliography • **60**

Index • **62**

Primary Source List • **63**

NTRODUCTION

EARLY SUPPORTERS OF WOMEN'S RIGHTS

While America fought for its freedom from Great Britain, and the Constitution was written declaring the freedoms and rights of its citizens, women were not allowed to vote, own property, get a divorce, serve on juries, or speak in public. In 1776, a woman voiced strong opinions about her desire to take a more prominent role in making decisions about how the government was run and share a voice in electing the people that ran it. Abigail Adams, the wife of the second president of the United States, wrote a letter to her husband, John Adams, expressing her reaction to the statement that "all men are created equal" after reading a draft of the Constitution written by the Second Continental Congress. In the letter, Abigail Adams wrote:

In a letter written to the *Sangamon Journal* in 1836, Abraham Lincoln, a young lawyer in Illinois, said that he believed all white people should have the right to vote as long as they were willing to carry the responsibilities of making decisions for the government of the United States. These responsibilities included paying taxes and going to war. Lincoln also added that this "right of suffrage" should not exclude females.

This quote was later used in fliers (such as the one shown on page 5) distributed by members of the Equal Franchise Society, a state-by-state organization that worked to change the laws and give women the right to vote. The name of the *Sangamon Journal* was misspelled in the flier, probably because the article was very old by the time the quote was used by women's rights supporters.

Equal Franchise Society

Legislative Series

"I go for all sharing the privileges of the government who assist in bearing its burdens. Consequently, I go for admitting all whites to the right of suffrage who pay taxes or bear arms, (by no means excluding females.")

Abraham Lincoln in a letter to the Sagamon Journal June 31, 1836.

I desire you would remember the Ladies, and do not put such unlimited power into the hands of Husbands, remember all men would be tyrants if they could, if particular care and attention is not paid to the Ladies we are determined to foment a Rebellion, and will not hold ourselves bound by any Laws in which we have no voice, or Representation.

Abigail Adams warned against giving all the power to men when forming a new government. She also believed that the rights and freedoms written in the Constitution should apply to women. At this point in history, Adams's letter did not change the meaning of the phrase "all men are created equal," and it did not immediately change the role of women in society. Abigail Adams believed that women would unite one day to secure equal rights for themselves.

By the early nineteenth century, more people shared the views that Adams had expressed many years before. During this time, new ideas were discussed and old ones were changing. Men and women alike reacted against slavery in the United States. Frances Wright, an early supporter of antislavery causes and rights for women, traveled throughout the country in 1827, daring to give speeches about these issues. She wrote articles and edited a newspaper called the *Free Enquirer*. While many people did not accept her ideas, she provided inspiration for many women who ultimately followed in her footsteps. About the same time, female abolitionists Angelina and Sarah Grimke traveled to cities in the Northeast and courageously spoke in public about their political views. Among the first abolitionists to make the connection between antislavery issues and women's rights, the Grimkes, Frances Wright, and many others like them, encouraged women to stand up for what they believed.

TIMELINE

March 31, 1776 — Abigail Adams writes a letter to her husband, President John Adams, asking that he "remember the ladies" when the Second Continental Congress writes the new Constitution of the United States of America.

1833 — Lucretia Mott is elected president of the first Female Anti-Slavery Society of Philadelphia.

1837 — Two hundred women attend the Women's Anti-Slavery Convention in New York City. It is the first national political meeting of women in New York. Eighty-one delegates from twelve states attend.

June 20, 1840 — Mott and other female delegates attend the World Anti-Slavery Convention in London. Women delegates are told to sit in the gallery and are not allowed to participate. Lucretia Mott and Elizabeth Cady Stanton meet.

July 19–20, 1848 — Three hundred people attend the first Woman's Rights Convention in Seneca Falls, New York. The Declaration of Sentiments and Declaration of Resolutions based on the Declaration of Independence are signed. These documents outline the main objectives for the

(continued on page 8)

TIMELINE

women's rights movement. This convention marked the beginning of others held like it throughout the country for years to come.

1851 — Sojourner Truth gives a speech called "Ain't I a Woman?" at the Woman's Rights Convention in Akron, Ohio.
Elizabeth Cady Stanton and Susan B. Anthony meet for the first time and begin their fifty-year partnership working for women's rights and suffrage.

May 23, 1852 — Elizabeth Cady Stanton and Susan B. Anthony start an organization called the Women's New York Temperance Society.

1855 — Elizabeth Cady Stanton gives her famous speech to the New York legislature asking for the passage of the Women's Suffrage Bill to allow for a law covering women's property rights.

1861 — The American Civil War begins. Many women work hard to support the war effort and put women's rights issues on hold until the war ends in 1865.

TIMELINE

May 10, 1866 — The American Equal Rights Association is founded by Susan B. Anthony, Elizabeth Cady Stanton, Lucretia Mott, and Lucy Stone. Lucretia Mott heads the organization that has merged members of the suffragists and the American Anti-Slavery Association.

January 8, 1868 — Elizabeth Cady Stanton and Susan B. Anthony publish the first issue of a women's rights newspaper called *The Revolution*.

July 28, 1868 — The Fourteenth Amendment is passed and women are not given the right to vote. This amendment grants citizenship to male African Americans but not to women. Many strong activists such as Susan B. Anthony and Elizabeth Cady Stanton strongly oppose its passage because it defines citizens as "male."

May 1869 — The women's rights movement splits into two groups over disagreements about the Fourteenth Amendment. The National Woman Suffrage Association, based in New York, is formed by Susan B. Anthony and Elizabeth

(continued on page 10)

TIMELINE

Cady Stanton, Lucy Stone, Henry Blackwell, and Julia Ward Howe organize the American Woman Suffrage Association, based in Boston.

November 9, 1869 — The territory of Wyoming is the first to grant unlimited suffrage to women.

February 3, 1870 — The Fifteenth Amendment is passed giving black men the right to vote

November 5, 1872 — Susan B. Anthony is arrested for attempting to vote in a presidential election.

1890 — The National Woman Suffrage Association and the American Woman Suffrage Association merge to form the National American Woman Suffrage Association. Elizabeth Cady Stanton becomes the organization's new president.

1895 — Elizabeth Cady Stanton publishes "The Women's Bible," a critical evaluation of the Bible's treatment of women. The NAWSA formally opposes Stanton's views.

TIMELINE

1900 — Susan B. Anthony resigns as president of the National American Woman Suffrage Association. Carrie Chapman Catt becomes the next president of this organization

March 3, 1913 — Alice Paul organizes a women's suffragist march in Washington, D.C. More than 5,000 women attend.

1919 — The United States House of Representatives votes to enfranchise women for the third time. The Senate passes the Nineteenth Amendment, and suffragists begin their state-by-state ratification campaign.
The name of the NAWSA is changed to the League of Women Voters.

August 18, 1920 — The Nineteenth Amendment, called the Susan B. Anthony Amendment, is ratified allowing women in the United States the unlimited right to vote.

CHAPTER 1

WOMEN'S INFLUENCE ON EARLY SOCIAL REFORM MOVEMENTS

The Anti-Slavery Society, founded in 1833 by William Lloyd Garrison, believed in freedom for all slaves in the United States. Garrison also believed that women should have the same rights as men. Lucretia Mott, a Quaker minister and abolitionist, became a member of the group and founded the Female Anti-Slavery Society of Philadelphia the same year. Garrison and Mott believed it was important for black and white women to have equal access to education and employment, the right to own property, and the right to have custody of their children. In many ways, these basic rights were similar to the rights that the Anti-Slavery Society fought to gain for slaves. Although the

This is a three-quarter-length portrait photograph of Lucretia Mott taken later on in her life. This formal photograph portrays Mott dressed in modest clothing. She comes across as a strong and dignified woman. Mott's determination to make a difference as an abolitionist and supporter of women's rights issues and her gentle manner of dealing with people made her a key figure in the establishment and organization of the women's rights movement. She remained active in the women's rights movement and attended the thirtieth anniversary of the Seneca Falls Convention at the age of eighty-five.

Anti-Slavery Society was initially run by men, women soon took major roles that gave them opportunities to speak and write about their objections to slavery and take an active role in a political organization. Women's involvement in the antislavery movement grew stronger as they continued to claim their right to participate with men in social reformation.

In 1840, Lucretia Mott and other women from the Anti-Slavery Society were chosen to attend the World Anti-Slavery Convention in London, England, with the male delegates. When they arrived, the British abolitionists voted to exclude the women. They were asked to sit in the gallery and observe the events, but they were not allowed to participate. William Lloyd Garrison sat with the women in protest of their exclusion from the convention and argued on their behalf. He believed that women should share equal roles as speakers and officers of the organization. Daniel O'Connell, a member of the British Parliament, and William Howitt, a British writer, wrote letters to Lucretia Mott opposing the decision to exclude women and offered their support.

Lucretia Mott met Elizabeth Cady Stanton at this convention. Stanton later became one of the most influential leaders of the women's movement. After they were denied the right to participate in the convention, Mott and Stanton spent the rest of their time formulating ideas for the first women's rights convention. Although the first women's convention did not take place until eight years after Stanton and Mott first discussed it, they both worked for causes related to women's rights from 1840 to 1848. Mott became more active in the women's antislavery society and continued to write and speak about equal rights for women. Stanton gave public speeches and spoke to members of the New York legislature in an attempt to change laws and allow married women to own their own property and keep their own earnings in New York State.

Historians believe that Mott and Stanton were greatly influenced by the traditions of the Iroquois Nation in upstate New York. They observed Iroquois women exercising their right to own property and the right to vote. There are many similarities between the Iroquois women's rights and the principles later incorporated into the framework of the women's rights movement. Through their participation in the Anti-Slavery Society, their experiences with their Iroquois counterparts, and exclusion from male-dominated organizations, Mott and Stanton finally put their plans into action in 1848.

Elizabeth Cady Stanton, Lucretia Mott, Martha Wright, and Jane Hunt met at Mary Ann M'Clintock's home (pictured on the next page) in Waterloo, New York, on July 16, 1848, to organize the first Woman's Rights Convention. It was here in Mary's parlor, that the group went about the difficult task of establishing a forum for the women's rights movement and writing a formal statement to be presented at the convention. Stanton did the majority of the writing of the Declaration of Sentiments (the first page is shown on page 18), which outlined the basic premise for the convention— equal rights for women including the right to vote. The Declaration of Sentiments modeled the same structure as the Declaration of Independence. It included a list of eighteen grievances that the women thought were important to address. The Declaration of Resolutions demanded eleven specific resolutions such as the right for women to speak openly in public, the right to equal and fair treatment under the law, the right to hold higher positions in education, and most important, the right to vote. The Declaration of Resolutions demanded that women be recognized and treated

The M'Clintock House originally located in Waterloo, New York, was the house of Thomas and Mary Ann M'Clintock who came to the area in 1836 from Pennsylvania. As members of the Waterloo Quaker community, the M'Clintocks became active in the abolition and women's rights movements. The M'Clintock family lived in this two-story brick house for twenty years before returning to Pennsylvania. The Woman's Rights National Historic Park in Seneca Falls, New York, bought the M'Clintock House in 1985 and moved it to Seneca Falls with other famous historic sites of the women's rights movement such as the home of Elizabeth Cady Stanton and the Wesleyan Chapel.

as man's equal in all aspects of life, including marriage and divorce, the workplace, and as members of the community.

The first Woman's Rights Convention was held on July 19–20 in Seneca Falls, New York. The first page of an announcement about the convention is shown on page 18. Over three hundred people came. At least forty of those in attendance were men. Frederick Douglass, a former slave and abolitionist, spoke in support of all the resolutions, including the one that most people resisted, giving women the right to vote. He stated that without it, women would have no way to protect their rights or make changes in the laws. After much discussion and debate, the resolution stating that women should have the right to vote finally passed. By the end of the convention, sixty-eight women and thirty-two men signed the declaration.

Negative reactions were expressed all over the country by the press and some members of the clergy, who verbally attacked the organizers of the convention. Many of the people who had signed the declaration withdrew their names and support. Only the antislavery newspapers continued to write articles in favor of women's rights.

Florence S. Maskrey
Minnesota, Iowa

Section VIII No 1

No 16

THE FIRST CONVENTION

EVER CALLED TO DISCUSS THE

Civil and Political Rights of Women,

SENECA FALLS, N. Y., JULY 19, 20, 1848.

———

WOMAN'S RIGHTS CONVENTION.

———

A Convention to discuss the social, civil, and religious condition and rights of woman will be held in the Wesleyan Chapel, at Seneca Falls, N. Y., on Wednesday and Thursday, the 19th and 20th of July current; commencing at 10 o'clock A. M. During the first day the meeting will be exclusively for women, who are earnestly invited to attend. The public generally are invited to be present on the second day, when Lucretia Mott, of Philadelphia, and other ladies and gentlemen, will address the Convention.*

———

* This call was published in the *Seneca County Courier*, July 14, 1848, without any signatures. The movers of this Convention, who drafted the call, the declaration and resolutions were Elizabeth Cady Stanton, Lucretia Mott, Martha C. Wright, Mary Ann McClintock, and Jane C. Hunt.

This call for the first Woman's Rights Convention was published without any signatures in the *Seneca County Courier* on July 14, 1848, five days before the convention. The announcement invited only women to attend on the first day and asked the general public to attend on the second day to hear Lucretia Mott address the convention.

2

DECLARATION OF SENTIMENTS.

When, in the course of human events, it becomes necessary for one portion of the family of man to assume among the people of the earth a position different from that which they have hitherto occupied, but one to which the laws of nature and of nature's God entitle them, a decent respect to the opinions of mankind requires that they should declare the causes that impel them to such a course.

We hold these truths to be self-evident : that all men and women are created equal ; that they are endowed by their Creator with certain inalienable rights, that among these are life, liberty, and the pursuit of happiness ; that to secure these rights governments are instituted, deriving their just powers from the consent of the governed. Whenever any form of government becomes destructive of these ends, it is the right of those who suffer from it to refuse allegiance to it, and to insist upon the institution of a new government, laying its foundation on such principles, and organizing its powers in such form as to them shall seem most likely to effect their safety and happiness. Prudence, indeed, will dictate that governments long established should not be changed for light and transient causes ; and accordingly, all experience hath shown that mankind are more disposed to suffer, while evils are sufferable, than to right themselves by abolishing the forms to which they were accustomed. But when a long train of abuses and usurpations, pursuing invariably the same object evinces a design to reduce them under absolute despotism, it is their duty to throw off such government, and to provide new guards for their future security. Such has been the patient sufferance of the women under this government, and such is now the necessity which constrains them to demand the equal station to which they are entitled.

The history of mankind is a history of repeated injuries and usurpations on the part of man toward woman, having in direct object the establishment of an absolute tyranny over her. To prove this, let facts be submitted to a candid world.

Elizabeth Cady Stanton read the Declaration of Sentiments on the first day of the Woman's Rights Convention. The Declaration of Sentiments demanded the same rights for women that men asked for in the Declaration of Independence. The Declaration of Sentiments specifically outlined facts and opinions about women's roles in society and gave the reasons and justification for the demands included in a second document called the Declaration of Resolutions.

CHAPTER 2

Sojourner Truth, a former slave, gained her freedom in 1827. She joined the abolitionist movement and traveled throughout the United States speaking out against slavery and supporting women's rights. Her speeches inspired many people to fight for universal suffrage for blacks and women.

LEADERS OF THE WOMEN'S RIGHTS MOVEMENT IN THE 1850s

During the 1850s, women's rights conventions offered a forum for the discussion of women's rights issues, which often turned into heated debates over human rights issues. Prominent leaders of the movement emerged by the mid-1850s. Lucy Stone mesmerized audiences with her eloquent speaking style. With her sharp mind and skill as a writer, Elizabeth Cady Stanton produced speeches, petitions, and articles that provided the written framework for the organization. Susan B. Anthony provided the drive and organizational skills needed to

Sojourner Truth listened quietly to speakers at an Ohio women's rights convention in 1851. In response to negative comments about women and the opinion that they may not be as smart as men, Sojourner Truth gave a fiery and memorable speech that later came to be known as "Ain't I a Woman?" The text of the speech is shown on the next page. A contemporary English translation is on page 51.

"Wall, chilern, whar dar is so much racket dar must be somethin' out o'kilter. I tink dat 'twixt de niggers of de Souf and de womin at de Norf, all ,talkin' 'bout rigts, de white men will be in a fix pretty soon. But what's all dis here talkin' 'bout?

"Dat man ober dar say dat womin needs to be helped into carriages, and lifted ober ditches, and to hab de best place everywhar. Nobody eber helps me into carriages, or ober mud-puddles, or gibs me any best place!" And rising herself to her right arm to the shoulder, showing her tremendous muscular power). I have ploughed, and planted, and gath-ered into barns, and no man could head me! And a'n't I a woman? I could work as much and eat as much as a man--when I could get it --and bear de lash as well! And a'n't I a woman? I have borne thirteen chilern, and seen'em mos' all sold off to salvery, and when I cried out with my mother's grief, none but Jesus heard me! And a'n't I a woman?

"Den dey talks 'bout dis ting in de head; what dis dey call it?" ("Intellect," whispered some one near.) "Dat it, honey. What's dat got to do wid womin's rights or nigger's rights? If my cup won't hold but a pint, and yourn holds a quarts, wouldn't ye be mean not to let me have my lit-tle half-measure full?" And she pointed her significant finger, and sent a keen glance at the minster who had made the arguement. The cheering was long and loud.

"Den dat little man in black dar, he say women can't have as much rights as men, 'cause Christ wan't a woman! Whar did your Christ come from?" Rolling thunder couldn't have stilled that crowd, as did those deep, wonderful tones, as she stood there with outstretched arms and eyes of fire. Raising her voice still louder, she re-peated, "What did your Christ come from? From God and a woman! Man had nothin' to do wid Him." oh, what a rebuke was to that little man.

Turning again to another objector, she took up the defense of Mother Eve. I can not follow her through it all. It was pointed and witty, and solemn; elicting at almost every sentence deafening applause; and by asserting; "If de fust woman God ever made was strong enough to turn de world upside down all alone, deses women together (and she glanced her eye over the platform) ought to be able to turn it back, and get it right side up again! And now dey is asking to do it, de men better let'em." Long-continued cheering greeted this. "Bleeged to ye for hearin' on me, and now old Sojourner han't got nothn' more to say."

This three-quarter-length portrait of Sojourner Truth taken some time in 1864, shows her standing, wearing spectacles, a shawl, and a peaked cap. Her right hand rests on a cane and she is carrying a satchel on her left arm. Sojourner Truth traveled all over the country giving speeches about women's rights. In order to support herself she sold postcards with her picture and the following quote, "I will sell the shadow to support the substance."

keep the women's movement heading in the right direction. Anthony traveled extensively around the country, delivering speeches that were written by Stanton. Together, these women and many others like them devoted much of their time and effort to gain more attention and support for women's rights.

As vice president of the second Woman's Right's Convention in 1853, William Lloyd Garrison gave a speech expressing his strong opinions about women's rights and those that opposed them. Although many people thought that Garrison's views on antislavery and women's rights were too radical for the time, he continued to fight for justice and equal rights throughout his life.

20 REPORT.

mind to overcome them. Perhaps this science too might be simplified until it came within our reach. I concur fully in the wish that those who are against, as well as those who are for us, will come here and speak their sentiments. I hope and believe they will be courteously received, and earnestly desire that they may give themselves up to the guidance of the truth which may be here elicited, no matter how much it may jar with their preconceived opinions. In conclusion, I hope there will be no long speeches, but that all that may be said shall be terse, and directed plainly to the subjects before the Convention."

OLIVER JOHNSON.—"I move that the limitation of time be adopted by the Convention."

(Motion seconded and passed.)

The Session closed at 12½ p. m.

FIRST DAY.

Afternoon Session.

The Session opened at 3, p. m.

The Resolutions adopted at the last Session being read,

WM. LLOYD GARRISON spoke thus:

"In view of the many able and earnest spirits assembled at this Convention, I am glad that it has been resolved that speakers shall occupy no more than twenty minutes; and yet it is obvious, that in the brief space of twenty minutes, it is utterly impossible to begin and complete an argument in regard to the great question which has thus brought us together.

But, having no time for preliminaries, the first pertinent question here is, what has brought us together? Why have we come from the East and from the West, and from the North? I was about to add, and from the South; but the South, alas! is so cursed by the spirit of slavery, that there seems to be no vitality left them in regard to any enterprise, however good, and the South cannot be represented on an occasion like this. It is because justice is outraged. We have met to protest against proud, rapacious, inexorable usurpation. What is this usurpation? What is this oppression of which we complain? Is it local? Does it pertain to the City of New York, or to the Empire State? No! It is universal—broader than the Empire State—broader than our national

This is a portion of the speech that William Lloyd Garrison presented at the Woman's Rights Convention in September 1853. In his speech, Garrison defends the right of women to share in the decision-making process with men in all levels of local, state, and national government. Garrison also urges women to continue to fight for an equal voice in making their own laws and choosing their own lawmakers.

CHAPTER 3

ELIZABETH CADY STANTON MAKES A DIFFERENCE

Stanton's work in the women's rights movement with her longtime friend Susan B. Anthony lasted over fifty years. During the 1850s and 1860s, Stanton lobbied for women's rights to a higher education and to a legal identity that included the right to own property and obtain a divorce. Stanton served as president of the National Woman Suffrage Association from 1869 to 1890. After raising seven children, Stanton continued to share her knowledge and opinions by giving lectures on family and child-rearing issues, abolition, temperance, and women's suffrage until her death at the age of eighty-seven.

After the Civil War broke out in 1861, women put their efforts into winning the war and abolishing slavery. Many women ran their homes or businesses alone and became more independent while men were away at war. Women devoted their time to the

On the facing page is a photograph created sometime between 1890 and 1910 of a daguerreotype taken in 1856 of Elizabeth Cady Stanton and her daughter, Harriot. A daguerreotype is an early photograph produced on a silver or silver-covered copper plate. Elizabeth's daughter, Harriot, grew up to carry on the work of her mother in the women's rights movement.

Elizabeth Cady Stanton and
her daughter, Harriot.
from a daguerreotype 1856

New-York, December 26, 1865.

Dear Friend:

As the question of Suffrage is now agitating the public mind, it is the hour for Woman to make her demand.

Propositions have already been made on the floor of Congress to so amend the Constitution as to exclude Women form a voice in the Government.* *As this would be to turn the wheels of legislation backward, let the Women of the Nation now unitedly protest against such a desecration of the Constitution, and petition for that right which is at the foundation of all Government, the right of representation.*

Send your petition, when signed, to your representative in Congress, at your earliest convenience.

Address all communications to

Standard Office, 48 Beekman St., New York.

In behalf of the National W. R. Com.

E. CADY STANTON,
S. B. ANTHONY,
LUCY STONE.

---

* See Bill of Mr. Jenckes, of Rhode Island.

Elizabeth Cady Stanton, Susan B. Anthony, and Lucy Stone drew up this petition on December 26, 1865, and sent it to women all over the country. Women were asked to write to their representatives in Congress in reference to the pending Fourteenth Amendment, which excluded women's suffrage. The addition of the word "male" in the Fourteenth Amendment applied only to gaining citizenship for black males and not for women.

war effort and put any further political action for women's rights on hold until the war ended in 1865. After the North won the war, abolitionists continued fighting for slaves to gain the right to vote.

The Thirteenth Amendment was passed in 1865 giving freedom to all slaves. Soon after, the pending ratification of the Fourteenth Amendment caused disagreements between abolitionists and women's rights activists. The purpose of the Fourteenth Amendment was to protect the freed slaves and guarantee them rights as citizens of the United States. However the language in the Fourteenth Amendment defined citizens as "males." Strong women's rights supporters like Stanton and Anthony did not support the Fourteenth Amendment because it did not include women as citizens and therefore kept them from securing the right to vote. Anthony and Stanton lost long-time supporters like William Lloyd Garrison and Fredrick Douglass, who felt it was important that black men be given the same rights as other men and did not want this issue to become entangled with the women's rights movement. Stanton, Anthony, and Lucy Stone sent out a petition (shown on page 26) asking women to write to Congress. Regardless, the Fourteenth Amendment was ratified in 1868.

In 1869, the mainstream suffrage movement split into two groups over these disagreements. Stanton and Anthony founded the National Woman Suffrage Association, dedicated to fighting for women's suffrage. Stone headed the American Woman Suffrage Association. Stanton and Anthony, who had fought so long and hard for both issues, insisted that women's suffrage be included in the Fifteenth Amendment to the Constitution. The Fifteenth Amendment was passed in 1870, stating that all citizens (men) of the United States could not be denied the right to vote based on race or color. Once again, women's suffrage was excluded.

A PETITION

FOR

UNIVERSAL SUFFRAGE.

To the Senate and House of Representatives:

The undersigned, Women of the United States, respectfully ask an amendment of the Constitution that shall prohibit the several States from disfranchising any of their citizens on the ground of sex.

In making our demand for Suffrage, we would call your attention to the fact that we represent fifteen million people—one half the entire population of the country—intelligent, virtuous, native-born American citizens; and yet stand outside the pale of political recognition.

The Constitution classes us as "free people," and counts us *whole* persons in the basis of representation; and yet are we governed without our consent, compelled to pay taxes without appeal, and punished for violations of law without choice of judge or juror.

The experience of all ages, the Declarations of the Fathers, the Statute Laws of our own day, and the fearful revolution through which we have just passed, all prove the uncertain tenure of life, liberty and property so long as the ballot—the only weapon of self-protection—is not in the hand of every citizen.

Therefore, as you are now amending the Constitution, and, in harmony with advancing civilization, placing new safeguards round the individual rights of four millions of emancipated slaves, we ask that you extend the right of Suffrage to Woman—the only remaining class of disfranchised citizens—and thus fulfil your Constitutional obligation "to Guarantee to every State in the Union a Republican form of Government."

As all partial application of Republican principles must ever breed a complicated legislation as well as a discontented people, we would pray your Honorable Body, in order to simplify the machinery of government and ensure domestic tranquillity, that you legislate hereafter for persons, citizens, tax-payers, and not for class or caste.

For justice and equality your petitioners will ever pray.

NAMES.	RESIDENCE.
Elisaby Stanton	New York
Susan B. Anthony	Rochester — N.Y.
Antoinette Brown Blackwell	New York
Lucy Stone	Newark N. Jersey
Joanna S. Morse	48 Livingston. Brooklyn
Ernestine L Rose	New York
Harriet E Eaton	6. West 14th Street N.Y
Catharine C Wilkeson	83 Clinton Place New York
Elizabeth R. Tilton	48 Livingston St. Brooklyn
Mary Fowler Gilbert	295 W. 19th St New York
Mary E Gilbert	New York
M. Griffith	New York.

In 1866, Elizabeth Cady Stanton, Susan B. Anthony, and Lucy Stone wrote "A Petition for Universal Suffrage" to Congress asking for an amendment to the Constitution that would not allow any state to disenfranchise any citizen because of his or her sex. They hoped to convince Congress to pass suffrage for women and black men at the same time. Congressman Thaddeus Stevens submitted this petition to Congress on January 29, 1866. This petition is signed at the bottom by some of the most famous and influential women suffragists of the women's rights movement, including Elizabeth Cady Stanton, Susan B. Anthony, Antoinette Brown Blackwell, Ernestine L. Rose, and others.

The Revolution, a weekly women's rights newspaper first published in Rochester, was owned by Susan B. Anthony and edited by Elizabeth Cady Stanton and Parker Pillsbury. The newspaper served as the platform for the National Woman Suffrage Association and it discussed issues such as discrimination against women in the workplace and divorce. Ten thousand copies of *The Revolution* were first published on January 8, 1868. Frustrated by their efforts to stop the passage of the Fourteenth Amendment because it did not include women in its definition of citizens, Stanton and Anthony took a strong stand for women's right to vote. Their views were reflected by the masthead of the newspaper, "Principles, not policy: justice not favors. Men, their rights, and nothing more; Women, their rights, and nothing less."

In the April 23, 1868, issue of *The Revolution*, under a section of the newspaper entitled, "What the Press Thinks Of Us," Miles O'Reilly wrote an article called "Brains, Bonnets, Babies and Ballots." In it, he discusses his opinion that women should devote their time and energy to taking care of their children rather than fighting for women's suffrage and worrying about the latest fashions. "It seems almost incredible that as a matter of choice women should prefer the luxury of wielding a ballot to that of nursing a baby." A portion of the reply written by one of *The Revolution*'s editors can be found on page 52. In it, O'Reilly's opinions are challenged. He is asked to see women as strong individuals who not only spend time running a household, teaching dignity and self-respect to their children, but also as active citizens who make time to get involved in charity work and social reform. "These women dress plainly, live simply, understand the science of government, political, and domestic economy, and are at the moment the salt of the nation." The ideas voiced by both sides were reflective of the conflicting opinions people had about women's roles in society during this time.

The Revolution.

PRINCIPLE, NOT POLICY: JUSTICE, NOT FAVORS.—MEN, THEIR RIGHTS AND NOTHING MORE: WOMEN, THEIR RIGHTS AND NOTHING LESS.

VOL. I.—NO. 16.　　　NEW YORK, THURSDAY, APRIL 23, 1868.　　　$2 A YEAR. SINGLE COPY 10 CENTS.

The Revolution.

ELIZABETH CADY STANTON, } Editors.
PARKER PILLSBURY,

SUSAN B. ANTHONY, Proprietor.

OFFICE 37 PARK ROW (ROOM 17).

THEODORE DREAMING, WITH FLAG AT HALF MAST.

LAST week's *Independent*, in a long column, throws Mr. Chase overboard, clears the track for Grant, and gets itself ready to wheel into line with the multitude in the coming contest. After the most unequivocal praise of "the Chief Justice," the "President of the Senate," "Salmon P. Chase," after making a profound bow to him in each of these capacities, admitting "that his life-long convictions have been in favor of liberty, justice and equality ; that he holds to the civil and political rights of all American citizens, without distinction of color or sex," Mr. Tilton winds up by withdrawing his advocacy of Mr. Chase for President now ends, because he has reason to believe that he would accept a nomination from the democratic party.

In the beginning of the new year the *Independent* unfurled its banner to the breeze with universal suffrage for all men and women, of every color and clime, inscribed thereon ; and this has been the editor's theme in all his lyceum lectures during the past winter, thus added to his personal admiration for the Chief Justice. Mr. Tilton occupies the same political platform with him, and that makes this sudden divorce the more extraordinary, assuming that the editor of a leading religious journal is governed in all things by moral principle.

There has been a little game going on in certain republican circles hostile to Chase, to prove that he always was a good democrat, and urging the democracy to take him up, thus to get one stumbling-stone out of the way of the Chicago Convention. The leaven, it seems, is beginning to work, and the *Independent* rushes bravely to the ramparts and hauls down the flag for Chase ; but this act, by its own showing, is by no means a logical sequence of its estimate of the man. But, unfortunately for all concerned, the wily democrats do not snap at the bait, and the republicans, with their Chief Justice, robes and all, are in as great a quandary as was the immortal Pickwick with the horse he feared to mount. From the standpoint of principle the question might be pertinent, why not follow a good man with the democratic party, rather than with the republicans help to place a drunken soldier in the White House ?

But, weary with the turmoil and disappointments of life, our youthful editor concludes as follows, and lies down to dream :

If at this late day it were not wholly useless to substitute another name, it might be the name of Charles Sumner, or Schuyler Colfax, or Ben Wade, or Gen. Butler. But, of course, the Chicago Convention will go pell mell for Gen. Grant. Nevertheless, we shall go on dreaming our day-dream of the happy day when only a great statesman shall be eligible to preside over the Great Republic.

This happy day is to be ushered in by teaching the people how to choose their leaders ; that the best interests of the nation do not depend on the success of any party, but on the virtue and education of the people. Why go "pell-mell" for Grant when all admit that he is unfit for the position ? It is not too late, if true men and women will do their duty, to make an honest man like Ben Wade President. Let us save the nation. As to the Republican party, the sooner that is scattered to the four winds of Heaven the better. If those who speak every week to 75,000 subscribers "dream" when they should be wide awake and at work, "a Great Republic to preside over" will soon be a dream also.　　E. C. S.

ANNA WIDE AWAKE WITH BANNERS FLYING.

THE heroic young orator, Anna E. Dickinson, spent several hours with us last week on her way to Western New York to fill a series of engagements, and promises us a day or two on her return.

The severity of her western work compelled her to rest a few days at home, but we are happy to say she is now herself again, and fulfilling her remaining appointments. We found her as earnest, prophetic and inspirational as ever, having no faith in Grant or the impeachment of the President by the republican party. This intuitive girl sees through all the political shams now going on at Washington. It may be well to delude THE PEOPLE, groaning under the effects of war and taxation, with the idea that this trial is to bring them some relief ; but those who see behind the scenes *know* that our present leaders have no appreciation of the nation's danger, or care for the necessities of the laboring classes.

The tyranny of capital and the narrow selfishness of the monied classes reveal a more hideous type of slavery than that of chattelism on the Southern plantation.

THE RADICAL IN A FOG.

THE *Radical*, reviewing Gail Hamilton's "Women's Wrongs, a Counter Irritant," says :

Our author has the rare merit of seeing both sides of a question, and having maintained most valiantly the right of woman to suffrage, she has the good sense to see and the fairness to allow, that the possession of the ballot will avail but little for the purposes which it is expected will be accomplished by it. For the admission of woman to the polls will not change the character, but only the volume of the vote upon any given question. Patrick may bring Biddy, his wife, to counterbalance Mrs. Percy Howard, and if there is any advantage, it will be on the side of Patrick, as the Biddies will be more easily led *en masse* than the more cultivated Mrs. Howards.

People who see two right sides to a question generally fail to see either side clearly. All questions of importance, such as relate to human rights, are so perfectly clear to those who see them at all, that both the right and the wrong side stand out in bold relief. It seems to us that neither Gail Hamilton nor her reviewer comprehends the deep significance of this question of universal suffrage. In reading this book we were struck with its weakness the moment the author lost sight of Todd and undertook to reason. Like the cat with a mouse, she was wide awake and intensely active until her victim was no more ; then came a reaction that left her foggy and dull through many intervening pages, until at the close she awoke from her nap and ascended into the higher realm of prophesy and speculation. After boldly asserting woman's right to suffrage, we were surprised at the flippant way in which she disposed of woman's duty and dignity in the exercise of their political rights. After annihilating the Rev. Todd and clearing the battle-ground of all she crush and rubbish of error, instead of rebuilding on the spot some marble pillar to the new idea, she sits down beside the dying Todd and confesses that although she has pierced him through and through to maintain woman's right to suffrage, yet its value in the regeneration of the race is not worth the strength she had spent to prove it. She was stung to action by Todd's insults to her sex. These she felt, but she did not perceive that what Todd said was the logical sequence of just such a public sentiment as she herself echoed in her foggy presentation of what her reviewer calls the other side of the question. The strongest way to maintain a right is to show the damage done in its denial. Now, if woman would not use the ballot, and be none the better for its possession, why contend for the right ? Why contend for the right to embrace a wolf when it would be folly or death to exercise it ?

The admission of woman to the polls will essentially change the character of our legislation, because then we shall have both the male and female idea represented in our laws and government. Force and selfishness will be incorporated with the higher, purer principles of love and sacrifice. "Biddy" will counterbalance with her loving mercy the stern justice of "Patrick," and "Mrs. Percy Howard," being a strong-minded, conscientious woman, will love her country as well as her household, and will feel the deepest interest in clearing up the great wilderness of life, in plucking the thorns from the ten thousand paths where her sons and daughters are soon to tread. When woman understands that all the abominations she sees at every turn—the rum hole, the brothel, the gambling-saloon—are subjects of legislation to be voted up or down, what stupidity to suppose that she will not gladly use her vote to remove temptation from the way of those she loves. Give us the right, gentlemen, and we

---

Even though *The Revolution* was popular with working-class women, it did not make a lot of money. By 1870, Susan B. Anthony had to pay $10,000 of her own money to pay off the debt for the newspaper. The focus of the newspaper changed when Anthony turned it over to Laura Curtis Bullard, who published the paper under this name until 1872. For a partial transcription, see pages 52–54.

will soon show you what class of women will govern this nation.

Nor will female suffrage affect the question of female labor. For the prices of labor must follow the laws of trade, and with these voting has nothing to do. But could legislation regulate the wages of labor, is there any reason to suppose, our author inquires, that woman would be more disposed than man to pay higher wages to women? Every one who has traded much with women will join in her "I fear not."

Legislation, war, taxation, nothing to do with the laws of trade! We recommend Gail and her reviewer to a deeper consideration of this whole question of political economy, and they will find that the political status of the laborer has a good deal to do with his work and wages. The ballot in the hands of the southern laborer changes the law of southern trade. Instead of the lash for his unrequited toil, he to-day works for wages, and makes his own contract. With the right to all the offices under government, to the colleges, law schools, theological seminaries, medical schools and hospitals, which the ballot gives, who does not see that the ranks of school teachers and sewing women would be thinned out at once, and the wages of those who remained necessarily increased? Whatever women might do for each other, the laws of trade will secure equal wages to all not depressed in the market by artificial conditions. What gives point to the strikes of working men? The ballot that lies behind them. Why are laborers more dignified in this country than in the Old World? Because they have a voice in the government with the ballot they hold in their hand, the key to all the advantages and opportunities of life.

Nor will the right to suffrage raise woman in the social scale. The intelligent, cultivated woman, stands no lower in her own eyes or in the eyes of men, because of her political disability. The frivolous and vain would not be elevated were the disability removed. The first does not need the ballot as an incentive to exertion and self-culture; and if the exciting questions of the times fail to arouse the apathy of the latter, it is to be feared that going to the polls would prove insufficient. "Mobs and rowdies have always voted, are mobs and rowdies still." The suggestion of the fat offices which the possession of the ballot would open to woman, Gail repels with an indignant "Get thee behind me, Satan."

The right of suffrage simply represents the divine idea of equality, taught in our new religion by Jesus, and echoed by the fathers in the theory of our government.

The moment you disfranchise any class you make an invidious distinction that degrades those thus ostracised, not only in their own eyes, but in the eyes of those in the superior position.

If women are not degraded in the eyes of men, how shall we account for the insulting laws on their statute books, their interpretations of Holy Writ—for Todd's pamphlet—for their treatment of our famous sculptor, Harriet Hosmer, who knocked in vain at the doors of their colleges for a course of lectures on anatomy—for their insolence to Dr. Mercy B. Jackson, in denying her the right to become a member of the Homœopathic Association of Physicians in Boston? Surely, these are not evidences of man's respect for woman. And if there are women in this nation who, knowing all these things, can read Coke, Blackstone, Story and Kent, without feeling the degradation of their whole sex, without an honest burst of indignation, we say they are lacking in the essential elements of true womanhood.

As to Gail's "Get thee behind me, Satan," we ask, would you rather be mistress of some fashionable roue, and live on his bounty, or postmistress on $5,000 a year, and live on your own industry, in virtue and independence? It is as honorable to serve the nation faithfully as it is the family and the home—no more, no less.

E. C. S.

WHAT THE PRESS SAYS OF US.

From the New York Citizen (Miles O'Reilly).

BRAINS, BONNETS, BABIES AND BALLOTS.

It will be an important step in the progress of society when women arrive at that state of mind which will induce them to pay more attention to their brains than to their bonnets, and to give more thought to their babies than to ballots. There is scarcely a doubt that the prevailing passion for fashionable display in dress absorbs much of the time which should be devoted to the improvement of the mind and to maternal duties. It has come to pass among women in our day, that the demands of fashion are inimical to the moral obligations imposed on the marriage state. The palpable duties of maternity are ignored for the frivolous gratification of frequenting the fashionable promenade in tight-fitting dresses and costly bonnets. The substantial treasures of the study are abandoned for the stupid frivolities of the boudoir, and society in consequence is overwhelmed with a nauseous flood of superficiality. It is idle to endeavor to conceal the vast amount of mischief effected in the world by the inordinate love of display that has grown up among us—carrying families down to ruin, and causing them to neglect many noble and virtuous duties.

Quite equal in its baleful effects on marital and social obligations is the passion for enfranchisement, at present animating the breasts of certain ladies with masculine proclivities. It seems almost incredible that as a matter of choice any woman should prefer the luxury of wielding a ballot to that of nursing a baby. The most potent source of woman's power is to be found in the nurture and training of her children, and the influence which a true woman will never fail to exert over her husband, her brother, or her friends. She will seldom seek in vain for noble representatives in these if she proves herself worthy of them. Then there are national considerations which the self-sacrifice of woman should not permit her to overlook. The country needs babies more than ballots, at this time; especially when we take into account our recent acquisitions from the negro ranks. It is of infinitely more importance that the ladies should have brains and babies than that they should flaunt bonnets and ballots. What say those talented and progressive ladies, including Parker Pillsbury, who edit "THE REVOLUTION?"

Now, Miles, pray do not mix things up in this unaccountable way. The strong and weak-minded have each their idiosyncrasies. To clear up your vision on this question, let us analyze and arrange for you the facts of life. On one side behold ballots, brains and babies. On the other, bonnets, balls, brocades, buchu and barrenness.

The women who demand the ballot are those who have brains and babies, who believe in one husband; in clean, comfortable, well-ordered homes; in healthy, happy children, and in the dignity and self-respect of those who serve the household—women who do not follow fashion or frivolity, but spend their leisure hours in works of charity and reform—in reading, writing, and healthy exercise. Every woman identified with our cause, except Susan B. Anthony, is married; nearly all have large families, and all alike are remarkable for vigor of mind and body. These women dress plainly, live simply, understand the science of government, political and domestic economy, and are at this moment the salt of the nation; trying to dignify labor and secure virtue, by urging on all women the duty of self-support; trying to purify and perpetuate the family relation, by pressing on men a new code of morals; trying to redeem the church by teaching practical Christianity; and trying to exalt the state by pressing on our statesmen the principles of justice and equality. Take a tour of inspection, Mr. O'Reilly, into the homes and habits of the "strong-minded," before you again allow your pen to lay at our doors any of the follies or vices of that class of women moulded after man's ideal.

Remember the supply is ever equal to the demand. In the vice, vacuity and vanity of the weak-minded women of our day, behold, oh! men of the republic, your own handiwork.

From the Convention-day Journal, St. Louis.

"THE REVOLUTION."—This paper, devoted to Woman's Rights principally, is having good success. Probably there are few Spiritualists but sympathize with and endorse the views of its editors on the question of Woman's Rights, and we are sure its largest patronage comes from the members of our societies. Our lecturers are the most eloquent agitators on that subject that it has. A few of them make it almost a specialty, doing great service in the cause.

Yes, the Spiritualists have done much to advance the cause of woman and every other cause, by leading people to think and examine for themselves. We have indeed a good list of subscribers from St. Louis.

From the Newburgh Daily Journal.

"THE REVOLUTION."—We have received the fourteenth number of this zealous and aggressive advocate of "Woman's Rights." It is edited by Mrs. Stanton and Parker Pillsbury, who battle away "manfully" for what they think justice requires to be added to the "womanly" stature. Every aspect of the subject is treated with vigorous ability, but, naturally, not always with discretion. It is believed, by this school of reformers, apparently, that their work is that of challenging public attention by the boldness and audacity of their innovations and pretensions, and not always to consider either the desirability or feasibility of the "reforms" for which they demonstrate. The consequence is that they often wound and retard the cause they would advance. "THE REVOLUTION," however, furnishes its readers much that is valuable, and gives to the advocates of the doctrines which it espouses the advantage of having them presented by able writers and through a medium which must be recognized as authority upon these matters. "THE REVOLUTION" also grapples with public questions outside of those pertaining more especially to the "rights" and "wrongs" of woman, and discusses politics, finance, and social topics, of every aspect.

If all these friends who criticise our mode of warfare will "wound the cause" the same way we do, we shall soon have the world ablaze on the question. If you have any fault to find, tell us precisely what it is. If there are any flaws in arguments or principles, show them up. We hate generalisms and mysterious warnings and doubtings.

From the Laws of Life, Dansville, N. Y.

"THE REVOLUTION," is the name of a weekly paper started at the beginning of this year, which advocates "educated suffrage, irrespective of sex or color; equal pay to women for equal work; eight hours labor," etc. Mrs. Elizabeth Cady Stanton, the leading editor, is, by native talent, education and experience, as competent to treat such subjects as any woman living, in this or any other country.

From the Memorial and Rock, Plymouth, Mass.

"THE REVOLUTION."—This sprightly paper, under the management of Elizabeth Cady Stanton and Susan B. Anthony, is making quite a stir in journalism. It discusses public matters in a spicy manner, and proves conclusively that for caustic sharpness and pointed pungency, a woman's pen fully maintains the reputation of her tongue.

From the Schoharie Republican.

"THE REVOLUTION."—"Principle, not policy, justice, not favors. Men, their rights and nothing more: Women, their rights and nothing less." Such is the title and such the motto of the organ of the "Women's Rights" party. It is sprightly, spicy and readable. Edited by Elizabeth Cady Stanton and Parker Pillsbury; Susan B. Anthony, Proprietor.

From the New York Atlas.

"THE REVOLUTION" exhibits pluck as well as ability. The force and freedom with which it discusses topics of vital importance, that are too often tabooed by false delicacy, deserve the warmest praise.

"THE REVOLUTION."—A number of this paper has

CHAPTER 4

Susan B. Anthony and Elizabeth Cady Stanton spent many years writing about their ideas and opinions, giving speeches, and organizing the women's movement. By the early 1870s, despite all their hard work, laws still had not been passed that gave women the same rights as men.

SUSAN B. ANTHONY AND THE FIGHT FOR WOMEN'S SUFFRAGE

After being denied the right to vote in Pennsylvania in 1871, Carrie S. Burnham, a doctor and a teacher, took her case to the Supreme Court of Pennsylvania on April 4, 1873. She made a plea for her right to vote, stating that she met the legal definition of a "freeman" and citizen of the United States. The Supreme Court disagreed and denied Burnham's request, claiming that even though women were citizens this did not necessarily entitle

This is the cover of the pamphlet that contains Carrie S. Burnham's arguments before Chief Justice Read and Associate Justices Agnew, Sharswood, and Mercur about why she was entitled to vote. Also contained in this document are an appendix written by Hon. George Sharswood, a complete history of the case, and a compilation of the laws of Pennsylvania concerning the rights of women. Although her efforts to claim her right to vote as a citizen of the United States were unsuccessful, Burnham showed courage in her actions and helped draw attention to women's suffrage.

CITIZEN SUFFRAGE.

THE

ARGUMENT

OF

CARRIE S. BURNHAM

BEFORE

CHIEF JUSTICE READ, AND ASSOCIATE JUSTICES AGNEW, SHARSWOOD AND MERCUR,

OF THE

SUPREME COURT OF PENNSYLVANIA, IN BANC,

On the Third and Fourth of April, 1873.

WITH AN APPENDIX

CONTAINING THE OPINION OF

HON. GEORGE SHARSWOOD,

AND A COMPLETE HISTORY OF THE CASE.

ALSO,

A COMPILATION OF THE LAWS OF PENNSYLVANIA TOUCHING THE RIGHTS OF WOMEN.

PHILADELPHIA:

SEND ORDERS TO E. M. DAVIS, PRESIDENT

CITIZEN'S SUFFRAGE ASSOCIATION, 333 WALNUT STREET.

1873.

82

MISS ANTHONY—Yes, your honor, I have many things to say; for in your ordered verdict of guilty, you have trampled under foot every vital principle of our government. My natural rights, my civil rights, my political rights, my judicial rights, are all alike ignored. Robbed of the fundamental 'privilege of citizenship, I am degraded from the status of a citizen to that of a subject; and not only myself individually, but all of my sex, are, by your honor's verdict, doomed to political subjection under this, so-called, form of government.

JUDGE HUNT—The Court cannot listen to a rehearsal of arguments the prisoner's counsel has already consumed three hours in presenting.

MISS ANTHONY—May it please your honor, I am not arguing the question, but simply stating the reasons why sentence cannot, in justice, be pronounced against me. Your denial of my citizen's right to vote, is the denial of my right of consent as one of the governed, the denial of my right of representation as one of the taxed, the denial of my right to a trial by a jury of my peers as an offender against law, therefore, the denial of my sacred rights to life, liberty, property and—

JUDGE HUNT—The Court cannot allow the prisoner to go on.

MISS ANTHONY—But your honor will not deny me this one and only poor privilege of protest against this high-handed outrage upon my citizen's rights. May it please the Court to remember that since the day of my arrest last November, this is the first time that either myself or any person of my disfranchised class has been allowed a word of defense before judge or jury—

JUDGE HUNT—The prisoner must sit down—the Court cannot allow it.

them to vote. However, at this point in history, this ruling applied only to women.

Carrie S. Burnham eventually became an attorney and was admitted to both the Pennsylvania Supreme Court and the United States Supreme Court. Ultimately, she did not live to see women win the right to vote.

Susan B. Anthony also believed that women should have the right to vote. Anthony voted in a presidential election in 1872, to bring public support to the women's suffrage movement. She was arrested and put on trial for voting illegally. Anthony was found guilty of voting without the legal right, on June 19, 1873. She was denied an appeal for a new trial by jury and received a fine of $100.00, which she refused to pay. Anthony's effort to vote in an election gained more attention for the women's suffrage issue. Many people saw her as a troublemaker and ridiculed her for her beliefs. Public opinion never stopped Anthony's continued fight for women's rights issues throughout the country.

Account 1 of Susan B. Anthony's trial appeared in the *Rochester Democrat and Chronicle* on June 20, 1873. Account 2, written by Matilda Joslyn Gage, appeared in the *Kansas Leavenworth Times* on July 3, 1873. Account 3 is Susan B. Anthony's own written account of the trial. It is this account that is believed to be the most accurate. The account on the opposite page is a reply given by Susan B. Anthony, taken from Account 3, in response to the judge's question.

This full-length portrait photograph of Susan B. Anthony was taken sometime between 1880 and 1906. Anthony's pose portrays her as a dignified, determined, and intelligent woman. Anthony remained active in the National Woman Suffrage Association until she resigned at the age of eighty. She died in 1906 at the age of eighty-six.

CHAPTER 5

THE STRUGGLE FOR THE VOTE CONTINUES

Susan B. Anthony's trial brought renewed interest to the women's suffrage issue. Anthony continued speaking to groups across the country, hoping to unite women for a common cause: securing the right to vote. Stanton and Anthony traveled extensively during the 1870s and 1880s giving speeches and holding meetings in an effort to educate women about the need for a federal suffrage amendment. They spoke in small frontier towns and in big cities, anywhere they could find someone to listen. Traveling provided opportunities for Stanton and Anthony to meet many women's rights supporters at the local and state levels and to participate in individual state campaigns for suffrage. Anthony addressed legislatures and congressional committees hoping to gain political support for an equal rights amendment.

Anthony gave a speech called "Social Purity" (a portion of which is reprinted on page 38) in a Sunday afternoon Dime lecture course in 1875. Anthony stated the importance of men and women sharing equal rights, honors, and privileges in the workplace and in society. In order for women to have these rights,

Women, like men, must not only have "fair play" in the world of work and self-support, but, like men, must be eligible to all the honors and emoluments of society and government . . . And the only possible way to accomplish this great change is to accord to women equal power in the making, shaping and controlling of the circumstances of life. That equality of rights and privileges is vested in the ballot, the symbol of power in a republic. Hence, our first and most urgent demand—that women be protected in the exercise of their inherent, personal, citizen's right to a voice in the government, municipal, state, and national.

Susan B. Anthony presented a speech entitled, "Social Purity" at the Grand Opera House in Chicago on March 14, 1875. She spoke to a large crowd about the social problems of the time and how they affected women. Anthony emphasized that in order for women to make lasting changes in society they must be given the right to vote and the opportunity to share an equal voice in making decisions at all levels of the government. Because of Anthony's persuasive speaking style, her lectures convinced many people to support women's suffrage. In 1876, Anthony and Stanton wrote a Declaration of Rights for Women. They took it to the Fourth of July ceremonies at the Centennial Exposition in Philadelphia. After being denied permission to read it formally, Stanton and Anthony handed out copies to members of the crowd. Anthony later read the declaration to a large group that had formed outside to hear her speak. After enduring many years of criticism and hostility, Anthony eventually earned respect for her efforts to win equal rights for women and men in all facets of society.

Stanton believed that they must be given the opportunity and power to make these changes by voting in local, state, and national elections.

In 1877, Anthony collected petitions from twenty-six states—totalling 10,000 signatures—and asked Congress to consider passing an amendment for women's suffrage, but Congress did not acknowledge them. However, Anthony and Stanton did see some progress as the result of many years of hard work. By the late 1800s women had won the right to vote in school board and local elections across the United States. In 1878 Anthony wrote a federal suffrage amendment that was introduced in every Congress until women were granted the right to vote in 1920.

In 1890, the two main women's suffrage groups, the National Woman Suffrage Association and the American Woman Suffrage Association, reunited after a twenty-one year separation and became the National American Woman Suffrage Association. Stanton resigned as president in 1892 and Anthony took over this position until 1900. NAWSA leaders believed that the only way to win suffrage for all women was to work at gaining it one state at a time. If the majority of the states gained suffrage for women, then Congress would have to pass a federal amendment granting women's suffrage throughout the United States. The focus of NAWSA became getting the right to vote.

On January 17, 1892, Elizabeth Cady Stanton and other NAWSA members met with the Judiciary Committee of the House to ask for a women's suffrage amendment. Stanton read a speech she had written called "The Solitude of Self." The frontispiece of the speech is on page 42. Stanton discussed the

importance of a woman's individual and civil rights. The following is an excerpt from her famous speech: "The strongest reason why we ask for woman a voice in the government under which she lives, in the religion she is asked to believe; equality in social life, where she is the chief factor, a place in the trades and professions, where she may earn her bread is because of her birthright to self-sovereignty, because, as an individual, she must rely on herself . . ." Stanton talked about the fact that women were responsible for themselves and their actions. She believed that women should have equal rights as individuals and as citizens of the United States to make their own decisions. One step toward obtaining these equal rights for women was the right to vote.

However, some of Stanton's views on women's role in society were not always accepted by everyone. Stanton published "The Woman's Bible, Part 1" in 1895. The cover of this pamphlet is shown on page 43. This book was Stanton's view on how the Bible influenced women's roles in society. She felt that many teachings in the Bible discriminated against women and kept them from working together as equals with men. Stanton's interpretation of the Bible shocked and angered many women's rights activists as well as those opposed to women's suffrage. NAWSA made a public statement separating the goal of the

This is a three-quarter-length portrait of Elizabeth Cady Stanton (seated) and Susan B. Anthony (standing). It was taken sometime between 1880 and 1902. Stanton and Anthony published the first three volumes of *The History of Woman Suffrage* with Matilda Joslyn Gage in 1887. By 1890, Stanton and Anthony played major roles in the merging of the two women's suffrage groups into the National American Woman Suffrage Association.

ELIZABETH CADY STANTON

Born November 12, 1815, in Johnstown, N. Y.
Died October 26, 1902, in New York City

SOLITUDE OF SELF

Address Delivered by Mrs. Stanton

Before the

Committee of the Judiciary of the United States Congress

Monday, January 18, 1892

Elizabeth Cady Stanton delivered her famous "Solitude of Self" speech to the National American Woman Suffrage Association on January 18, 1892, when she resigned as president of the association. She also presented this speech to the United States House Committee on the Judiciary and to the United States Senate Committee. Stanton and others believed this was the best speech she had ever written. Susan B. Anthony said that Stanton's speech was "the strongest and most unanswerable argument and appeal ever made . . . for the full freedom and franchise of women." Ten thousand copies of Stanton's speech were later reprinted and distributed throughout the United States by Congress as a birthday centennial gift. Shown above is the cover of the "Solitude of Self" speech with a picture of Elizabeth Cady Stanton on the front. An excerpt of her speech is on page 54.

Price, 10 Cents
Twelve Copies for $1.00

Bible and Church Degrade

WOMAN

CONTENTS

		Page
I.	The Effect of Woman Suffrage on Questions of Morals and Religion,	1
II.	The Degraded Status of Woman in the Bible,	5
III.	The Christian Church and Woman,	11

BY

ELIZABETH CADY STANTON

H. L. GREEN, Publisher
Office of Free Thought Magazine, 213 East Indiana Street
CHICAGO, ILL.

"The Woman's Bible" was reprinted in 1898 and included an additional twenty-page pamphlet entitled "Bible and Church Degrade Woman." In the pamphlet, three essays were added that further explained Stanton's theories about religion. This is the cover of the twenty-page pamphlet, which sold for ten cents a copy.

organization from Stanton's personal opinions. "The Woman's Bible," unlike so many other of Stanton's articles and speeches, was never universally accepted.

From the late 1890s through 1910, NAWSA went through some major changes as new leaders of the women's movement became involved. Carrie Chapman Catt joined NAWSA in 1890 and worked actively to gain state-by-state suffrage. In 1894, Catt led the successful suffrage campaign in Colorado. By 1896, Wyoming, Colorado, Utah, and Idaho had gained full suffrage. Catt's enthusiasm and organizational skills strengthened NAWSA, inspired supporters, and brought in new members. She took over as president of NAWSA when Susan B. Anthony resigned in 1900. In 1904, Catt resigned her position, but remained active in the organization.

Harriot Stanton Blatch, Elizabeth Cady Stanton's daughter, worked hard to bring a new suffrage bill to both houses of the New York State legislature for debate. Blatch formed the Equality League of Self-Supporting Women in 1907, which became known as the Women's Political Union in 1910. Stanton actively organized campaigns, speakers, and pickets in order to gain attention for women's suffrage. Blatch's approach attracted many middle-class women who were new to the women's suffrage movement. Blatch organized open-air meetings and a large parade in which suffragists marched down Fifth Avenue in New York City on May 21, 1910. This parade was the first of many demonstrations organized to draw attention to women's suffrage. By 1916, the Women's Political Union merged with the Congressional Union, later known as the National Woman's Party, under the leadership of Alice Paul.

WOMAN SUFFRAGE HEADQUARTERS. MEN OF OHIO!
GIVE THE WOMEN A SQUARE DEAL
Vote For Amendment Nº 23 On September 3 – 1912.

COME IN AND LEARN WHY WOMEN OUGHT to Vote.

This is the women's suffrage headquarters on Upper Euclid Avenue in Cleveland, Ohio, in 1912. The smaller sign invites the people of Ohio to come in and learn why women should get the right to vote. The large sign encourages men to "give the women a square deal" by voting for Amendment Number 23 on September 3, 1912. This is one example of the state-by-state effort to win suffrage.

This is the official cover for the program that tells about the Woman Suffrage Procession held in Washington, D.C., on March 3, 1913. The cover shows a woman dressed in beautiful, ornate clothing and riding a horse. The woman is blowing a horn with a "Votes for Women" banner on it. The United States Capitol is in the background. The place of the march and the date are prominently displayed on the bottom right-hand side of the program.

In 1913, Alice Paul and supporters organized a suffragist march on Washington, D.C. that drew a crowd of 5,000 suffragists. In the hope of winning more public support for women's suffrage, the gathering was planned on the same day as Woodrow Wilson's presidential inauguration. However, the march drew a lot of controversy; army troops were later sent in to control an angry crowd of supporters and those who opposed them.

This victory map from 1917 shows the American states in which suffrage had been won by this point. This page was included in the "Women's Voter's Manual," written by Carrie Chapman Catt and published by the New York Century Company in 1918. It's interesting to note that by 1917, thirteen states had won full suffrage, mostly in the northwestern and southwestern parts of the United States. New York, Kansas, and Arkansas also had won full suffrage for women by this time. Many of the other states had partial or no suffrage by this time. Some states allowed women to vote only in presidential elections, while others allowed them to vote only in local elections or for school and bond issues. Other states allowed a limited combination of these. Before the passage of the Nineteenth Amendment in 1919, eleven states had granted full suffrage. Fourteen states gave women limited suffrage allowing them to vote only in local elections.

Tension within the movement continued to build as supporters grew impatient at the lack of progress. Carrie Chapman Catt, reelected as the NAWSA president in 1915, combined efforts with lobbying for a new federal amendment. Alice Paul organized pickets at the White House to make a plea for President Woodrow Wilson's support of the Nineteenth Amendment.

Paul believed that with President Wilson's support, the women's suffrage amendment would pass in Congress. Paul continued a series of protests that included picketing the White House and hunger strikes before President Wilson finally agreed to publicly support women's suffrage in 1918.

Known for the use of satire in her poems about women's suffrage, Alice Duer Miller wrote several poems (one is shown on page 49) that expressed her feelings about women being denied the right to vote. In the humorous poem, "Women," shown on the next page, Miller points out the strengths of women in obvious contrast to the stereotypes given to them by men. She also makes a strong point about why women should be given the right to vote. While women's rights activists struggled to make a difference by taking part in state-by-state campaigns to win the right to vote, many people like Alice Duer Miller became supporters and worked to change the minds of those that still opposed women's suffrage.

Finally on June 4, 1919, both the House of Representatives and the Senate agreed to pass the Nineteenth Amendment, also known as the Susan B. Anthony Amendment. Suffragists immediately went to work on a state-by-state ratification campaign for thirty-six states that lasted another fourteen months. In

ARE WOMEN PEOPLE?

Women

(With rather insincere apologies to Mr. Rudyard Kipling.)

I WENT to ask my government if they would set me free,
They gave a pardoned crook a vote, but hadn't one for me;
The men about me laughed and frowned and said: "Go home, because
We really can't be bothered when we're busy making laws."

Oh, it's women this, and women that and women have no sense,
But it's pay your taxes promptly when it comes to the expense,
It comes to the expense, my dears, it comes to the expense,
It's pay your taxes promptly when it comes to the expense.

I went into a factory to earn my daily bread:
Men said: "The home is woman's sphere."
  "I have no home," I said.
[74]

WOMEN'S SPHERE

But when the men all marched to war, they cried to wife and maid,
"Oh, never mind about the home, but save the export trade."

For it's women this and women that, and home's the place for you,
But it's patriotic angels when there's outside work to do,
There's outside work to do, my dears, there's outside work to do,
It's patriotic angels when there's outside work to do.

We are not really senseless, and we are not angels, too,
But very human beings, human just as much as you.
It's hard upon occasions to be forceful and sublime
When you're treated as incompetents three-quarters of the time.

But it's women this and women that, and woman's like a hen,
But it's do the country's work alone, when war takes off the men,
[75]

ARE WOMEN PEOPLE?

And it's women this and women that and everything you please,
But woman is observant, and be sure that woman sees.

Alice Duer Miller worked as a professional writer. As an advocate of the women's suffrage movement, she wrote a series of columns for the *New York Tribune* entitled "Are Women People?" Many of her poems, which were originally printed in her columns, were published by the George Doran Company in 1915 in a book entitled *Are Women People? A Book of Rhymes for Suffrage Times*. A sequel was published in 1917, and the title was changed to *Women Are People!* A transcription of the poem is on pages 54–55.

This photo from the National Photo Company Collection (Library of Congress), taken in 1917, shows three women casting their ballots for the first time, in an election in New York City. The following caption accompanied this photograph: "Calm about it. At Fifty-sixth and Lexington Avenue, the women voters showed no ignorance or trepidation, but cast their ballots in a businesslike way that bespoke of suffrage."

August 1920, after a long hard battle that took seventy-one years, the Nineteenth Amendment to the Constitution was adopted. Women finally had the right to vote!

PRIMARY SOURCE TRANSCRIPTIONS

Page 21: Ain't I a Woman?

CONTEMPORARY ENGLISH TRANSLATION

Ain't I a Woman?
by
Sojourner Truth
Delivered 1851
Women's Convention, Akron, Ohio

Well, children, where there is so much racket there must be something out of kilter. I think that between the negroes of the South and the women of the North, all talking about rights, the white men will be in a fix pretty soon. But what's all this here talking about?

That man over there says that women need to be helped into carriages, and lifted over ditches, and to have the best place everywhere. Nobody ever helps me into carriages, or over mud-puddles, or gives me any best place! And ain't I a woman? Look at me! Look at my arm! I have ploughed and planted, and gathered into barns, and no man could head me! And ain't I a woman? I could work as much and eat as much as a man—when I could get it—and bear the lash as well! And ain't I a woman? I have borne thirteen children, and seen most all sold off to slavery, and when I cried out with my mother's grief, none but Jesus heard me! And ain't I a woman?

Then they talk about this thing in the head; what's this they call it? [member of audience whispers, "intellect"] That's it, honey. What's that got to do with women's rights or negroes' rights? If my cup won't hold but a pint, and yours holds a quart, wouldn't you be mean not to let me have my little half measure full?

Then that little man in black there, he says women can't have as many rights as men, because Christ wasn't a woman! Where did your Christ come from? Where did your Christ come from? From God and a woman! Man had nothing to do with Him.

If the first woman God ever made was strong enough to turn the world upside down all alone, these women together ought to be able to turn it back, and get it right side up again! And now they are asking to do it, the men better let them.

Obliged to you for hearing me, and now old Sojourner has got nothing more to say.

Pages 30–31: *The Revolution*

TRANSCRIPTION

WHAT THE PRESS SAYS OF US.

From the New York Citizen (Miles O'Reilly).

BRAINS, BONNETS, BABIES AND BALLOTS.

It will be an important step in the progress of society when women arrive at that state of mind which will induce them to pay more attention to their brains than to their bonnets, and to give more thought to their babies than to ballots. There is scarcely a doubt that the prevailing passion for fashionable display in dress absorbs much of the time which should be devoted to the improvement of the mind and to maternal duties. It has come to pass among women in our day, that the demands of fashion are inimical to the moral obligations imposed on the marriage state. The palpable duties of maternity are ignored for the frivolous gratification of frequenting the fashionable promenade in the tight-fitting dresses and costly bonnets. The substantial treasures of the study are abandoned for the stupid frivolities of the boudoir, and society in consequence is overwhelmed with a nauseous flood of superficiality. It is idle to endeavor to conceal the vast amount of mischief effected in the world by the inordinate love of display that has grown up among us—carrying families down to ruin, and causing them to neglect many noble and virtuous duties.

Quite equal in its baleful effects on marital and social obligations is the passion for enfranchisement, at present animating the breasts of certain ladies with masculine proclivities. It seems almost incredible that as a matter of choice any woman should prefer the luxury of wielding a ballot to that of nursing a baby. The most potent source of woman's power is to be found in the nurture and training of her children, and the influence which a true woman will never fail to exert over her husband, her brother, or her friends. She will seldom seek in vain for noble representatives in these if she proves herself worthy of them. Then there are national considerations which the self-sacrifice of woman should not permit her to overlook. The country needs babies more than ballots, at this time; especially when we take into account our recent acquisitions from the negro ranks. It is of infinitely more importance that the ladies should have brains and babies than that they should flaunt bonnets and ballots. What say those talented and progressive ladies, including Parker Pillsbury, who edit "The Revolution?"

Now, Miles, pray do not mix things up in this unaccountable way. The strong and weak-minded have each their idiosyncrasies. To clear up your vision on this question, let us analyze and arrange for you the facts of life. On one side behold ballots, brains and babies. On the other, bonnets, balls, brocades, buchu and barrenness.

The women who demand the ballot are those who have brains and babies, who believe in one husband; in clean, comfortable, well-ordered homes; in healthy, happy children, and in the dignity and self-respect of those who serve the household—women who do not follow fashion or frivolity, but spend their leisure hours in works of charity and reform–in reading, writing, and healthy exercise. Every woman identified with our cause, except Susan B. Anthony, is married; nearly all have large families, and all alike are remarkable for vigor of mind and body. These women dress plainly, live simply, understand the science of government, political and domestic economy, and are at this moment the salt of the nation; trying to dignify labor and secure virtue, by urging on all women the duty of self-support; trying to purify and perpetuate the family relation, by pressing on men a new code of morals; trying to redeem the church by teaching practical Christianity; and trying to exalt the state by pressing on our statesmen the principles of justice and equality. Take a tour of inspection, Mr. O'Reilly, into the homes and habits of the "strong-minded," before you again allow your pen to lay at our doors any of the follies or vices of that class of women moulded after man's ideal.

Remember the supply is ever equal to the demand. In the vice, vacuity and vanity of the weak-minded women of our day, behold, oh! men of the republic, your own handiwork.

From the Convention-day Journal, St. Louis.

"The Revolution."—This paper, devoted to Woman's Rights principally, is having good success. Probably there are few Spritualists but sympathize with and endorse the views of its editors on the questions of Woman's Rights, and we are sure its largest patronage comes from the members of our societies. Our lecturers are the most eloquent agitators on the subject that it has. A few of the make it almost a specialty, doing great service in the cause.

Yes, the Spiritualists have done much to advance the cause of woman and every other cause, by leading people to think and examine for themselves. We have indeed a good list of subscribers from St. Louis.

From the Newburgh Daily Journal.

"The Revolution."—We have received the fourteenth number of this zealous and aggressive advocate of "Woman's Rights." It is edited by Mrs. Stanton and Parker Pillsbury, who battle away "manfully" for what they think justice requires to be added to the "womanly" stature. Every aspect of the subject is treated with vigorous ability, but, naturally, not always with discretion. It is believed, by this school of reformers, apparently, that their work is that of challenging public attention by the boldness and audacity of their innovations and pretensions, and not always to consider either the desirability or feasibility of the "reforms" for which they demonstrate. The consequence is that they often wound and retard the cause they would advance. "The Revolution," however, furnishes its readers much that is valuable, and gives to the advocates of the doctrines which it espouses the advantage of having them presented by able writers and through a medium which must be recognized as authority upon these matters. "The Revolution" also grapples with public questions outside of those pertaining more especially to the "rights" and "wrongs" of woman, and discusses politics, finance, and social topics, of every aspect.

If all these friends who criticise our mode of warfare will "wound the cause" the same way we do, we shall soon have the world ablaze on the question. If you have any fault to find, tell us precisely what it is. If there are any flaws in arguments or principles, show them up. We hate generalisms and mysterious warnings and doubtings.

From the Laws of Life, Dansville, N.Y.

"The Revolution," is the name of a weekly paper started at the beginning of this year, which advocates "educated suffrage, irrespective of sex or color; equal pay to women for equal work; eight hours labor," etc.

Mrs. Elizabeth Cady Stanton, the leading editor, is, by native talent, education and experience, as competent to treat these subjects as any woman living, in this or any other country.

From the Memorial and Rock, Plymouth, Mass.

"The Revolution."—This sprightly paper, under the management of Elizabeth Cady Stanton and Susan B. Anthony, is making quite a stir in journalism. It discusses public matters in a spicy manner, and proves conclusively that for caustic sharpness and pointed pungency, a woman's pen fully maintains the reputation of her tongue.

From the Schoharie Republican.

"The Revolution."—"Principle, not policy, justice, not favors. Men, their rights and nothing more: Women, their rights and nothing less." Such is the title and such the motto of the organ of the "Women's Rights" party. It is sprightly, spicy and readable. Edited by Elizabeth Cady Stanton and Parker Pillsbury; Susan B. Anthony, Proprietor.

From the New York Atlas.

"The Revolution" exhibits pluck as well as ability. The force and freedom with which it discusses topics of vital importance, that are too often tabooed by false delicacy, deserve the warmest praise.

Page 42: Elizabeth Cady Stanton's "Solitude of Self" Speech

TRANSCRIPTION

The isolation of every human soul and the necessity of self-dependence must give each individual the right to choose his own surroundings. The strongest reason for giving woman all the opportunities for higher education, for the full development of her faculties, forces of mind and body; for giving her the most enlarged freedom of thought and action; a complete emancipation from all forms of bondage, of custom, dependence, superstition; from all the crippling influences of fear, is the solitude and personal responsibility of her own individual life. The strongest reason why we ask for woman a voice in the government under which she lives; in the religion she is asked to believe; equality in social life, where she is the chief factor; a place in the trades and professions, where she may earn her bread, is because of her birthright to self-sovereignty; because, as an individual, she must rely on herself. No matter how much women prefer to lean, to be protected and supported, nor how much men desire to have them do so, they must make the voyage of life alone, and for safety in an emergency they must know something of the laws of navigation. To guide our own craft, we must be captain, pilot, engineer; with chart and compass to stand at the wheel; to match the wind and waves and know when to take in the sail, and to read the signs in the firmament over all. It matters not whether the solitary voyager is man or woman.

Page 49: Poem from *Are Women People? A Book of Rhymes for Suffrage Times*

TRANSCRIPTION

Woman
(With rather insincere apologies to Mr. Rudyard Kipling)

I WENT to ask my government if they would
set me free,
They gave a pardoned crook a vote, but
hadn't one for me;
The men about me laughed and frowned
and said: "Go home because,
we really can't be bothered when we're
busy making laws."

Oh, it's women this, and women that and
women have no sense,
But it's pay your taxes promptly when it
comes to the expense,
It comes to the expense, my dears, it comes
to the expense,
It's pay your taxes promptly when it comes
to the expense.
I went into a factory to earn my daily bread:
Men said:"The home is woman's sphere."
"I have no home," I said.
But when the men all marched to war, they
cried to wife and maid,
"Oh never mind about the home, but save
the export trade."

For it's women this and women that, and
home's the place for you,
But it's patriotic angels when there's outside
work to do.
There's outside work to do, my dears,
there's outside work to do,
It's patriotic angels when there's outside
work to do.
We are not really senseless, and we are not
angels, too,
But very human beings, human just as much as you.
It's hard upon occasions to be forceful and
sublime,

When you're treated as incompetent three-
quarters of the time.
But its women this and women that, and
woman's like a hen,
But it's do the country's work alone, when
war takes off the men,
And it's women this and women that and
everything you please,
But woman is observant, and be sure that woman sees.

GLOSSARY

abolitionist A person in favor of putting an end to something, such as an institution, custom, practice, or condition.

amendment A proposal made into a bill, law, or constitution.

Anti-Slavery Society An abolitionist group, formed in 1833 by William Lloyd Garrison, dedicated to ending slavery.

assembly A group of people gathered together for a common purpose.

civil rights Those rights guaranteed to a person by the Thirteenth, Fourteenth, Fifteenth, and Nineteenth Amendments to the Constitution and by other acts of Congress.

Congress The lawmaking body of the United States government consisting of the Senate and the House of Representatives.

consent To agree to do something.

constitution A document in which laws and principles of a government are written down. The United States Constitution, adopted in 1789, consists of seven articles and twenty-four amendments.

convention A meeting of members or representatives of a political, social, professional, or religious group.

daguerreotype An early type of photograph made with a plate of chemically treated metal or glass.

debate To take part in a formal discussion in which two different sides of a question are argued.

declaration A formal statement.

Declaration of Independence The formal statement written by Thomas Jefferson and adopted July 4, 1776, by the Second Continental Congress. This document stated that the thirteen colonies were independent of Great Britain.

delegate A person chosen to speak or act for others at a meeting or convention.

discriminate To treat or judge someone unfairly or take away his or her rights because of the person's race, class, or sex.

emancipation To set someone free.

flier A small printed notice that is passed out by hand.

foment To promote something.

forum A meeting or opportunity for open discussion.

Fourteenth Amendment An amendment to the United States Constitution ratified in 1868, granting citizenship to all male citizens.

grievance A formal complaint.

House of Representatives The lower branch of the legislature of the United States federal government.

legislature A group of people given the responsibility and power to make laws for a country or state.

lobby To try to persuade lawmakers to vote for or against an issue.

Nineteenth Amendment An amendment to the Constitution passed in 1920, giving women the right to vote.

petition A formal document that requests something from a person or group who has the power to change a situation. A petition is often signed by a number of people making the request.

political Relating to the government.

rebellion An organized resistance to the authority or government in power.

reformation A movement aimed at improving or changing social or political problems in the government or society.

representation The act of a person standing up for another person or group by speaking on his, her, or its behalf.

resolution A formal statement of opinion, directed at settling a disagreement, which is adopted by a group.

satire The use of words or actions to make something or someone look foolish.

sentiment An expression of feelings or opinions as a basis for taking a specific action.

suffrage The right to vote.

suffragist A person who speaks or writes on behalf of people who want the right to vote, especially women.

temperance A movement to control and end the sale of alcohol.

FOR MORE INFORMATION

Due to the changing nature of Internet links, the Rosen Publishing Group, Inc., has developed an online list of Web sites related to the subject of this book. This site is updated regularly. Please use this link to access the list:

http://www.rosenlinks.com/psah/wosu/

FOR FURTHER READING

Banner, Lois W. *Elizabeth Cady Stanton: A Radical for Women's Rights*. Boston, MA: Addison-Wesley Publishing, 1998.

Byrant, Jennifer Fisher. *Lucretia Mott: A Guiding Light*. Grand Rapids, MI: William B. Eerdmans Publishing Co., 1996.

Kendall, Martha E. *Susan B. Anthony: Voice for Women's Voting Rights*. Springfield, NJ: Enslow Publishing, 1997.

McKissack, Patricia, and Fredrick McKissack. *Sojourner Truth: Ain't I a Woman?* New York: Scholastic Paperbacks, 1994.

Stalcup, Brenda. *Susan B. Anthony* (People Who Made History). Farmington Hills, MI: Greenhaven Press, 2001.

# BIBLIOGRAPHY

Anthony Center for Women's Leadership. "History of Women's Suffrage." University of Rochester. 1999. Retrieved October 29, 2001 (http://www.rochester.edu/SBA/timeline1.html).

Byrant, Jennifer Fisher. *Lucretia Mott: A Guiding Light*. Grand Rapids, MI: William B. Eerdmans Publishing Co., 1996.

Connell, Kate. *They Shall Be Heard: Susan B. Anthony and Elizabeth Cady Stanton*. Austin, TX: Raintree/Steck-Vaughn, 1993.

Lucretia Mott's Reform Movement Networks. "How Did Lucretia Mott's Activism Between 1840 and 1860 Combine Her Commitments to Antislavery and Women's Rights?" Lucretia Coffin Mott Correspondence Project, Pamona College. Carol Faulkner and Beverly Wilson Palmer. May 1999. Retrieved December 14, 2001 (http://womhist.binghamton.edu/mott/intro.htm).

My History Is America's History. "About Women's History–Comprehensive Research." National Endowment for the Humanities (NEH). Project for the White House Millennium Council. William R. Ferris (chairman). November 1999. Retrieved January 4, 2002 (http://www.myhistory.org/historytopics/articles/suffrage.html).

PBS: *Not for Ourselves Alone. The Story of Elizabeth Cady Stanton and Susan B. Anthony*. "United States vs. Anthony." Excerpt from *Life and Work of Susan B. Anthony* by Ida Husted Harper (chapter 24). Retrieved December 1, 2001 (http://www.pbs.org/stantonanthony/resources/seneca_falls_bkgd.html).

Rutgers University. Documents by Stanton and Anthony: Stanton and Anthony Papers Project Online. "Address by Elizabeth Cady Stanton on Woman's Rights in 1848." Kimberly Banks. July 12, 1999. Retrieved January 2, 2002 (http://ecssba.rutgers.edu/docs.html).

Sagan, Miriam. *Women's Suffrage* (World History Series). San Diego, CA: Lucent Books, 1995.

Smith, Betsy Covington. *Women Win the Vote*. Englewood Cliffs, NJ: Silver Burdett Press, Inc., 1989.

University of Rochester. The Susan B. Anthony Center for Women's Leadership. "US Suffrage Movement Timeline." March 9, 2001. Retrieved December 7, 2001 (http://www.rochester.edu/SBA/timeline1.html).

Weatherford, Doris. *A History of the American Suffragist Movement*. Santa Barbara: CA: ABC-CLIO, Inc., 1998.

Women's History Powered by the History Net. "About Women's History—Comprehensive Research." Jone Johnson Lewis. 1999–2002. Retrieved December 29, 2001 (http://womenshistory.about.com/mbody.htm).

Women's Rights—Bios of Prominent American Women (Department, State, International, and Information Programs). Maintained by the U.S. Department of State. "Prominent American Women in the Women's Rights Movement." January, 25, 2001. Retrieved November 29, 2001 (http://usinfo.state.gov/usa/womrts/bios.htm).

Women's Studies Historical Timelines—Wstimeline4. Central Oregon Community College. "Part 4: Struggle for the Vote." Cora Agatucci, 1998. Retrieved January 3, 2002 (http://www.cocc.edu/cagatucci/classes/ws101/wstml/wstml4.htm).

INDEX

A

Adams, Abigail, 4-6, 7
Adams, President John, 4, 7
American Equal Rights Association, 9
American Woman Suffrage Association, 10, 27, 39
Anthony, Susan B., 8, 9, 10, 11, 20-22, 24, 27, 29, 32, 35, 37-39, 44, 48
Anti-Slavery Society, 7, 9, 12-14, 15

B

Blackwell, Henry, 10
Blatch, Harriot Stanton, 44
Burnham, Carrie S., 32-35

C

Catt, Carrie Chapman, 11, 44, 48
Civil War, 8, 24, 27

D

Declaration of Resolutions, 7, 15-17
Declaration of Sentiments, 7, 15
Douglass, Frederick, 17, 27

F

Free Enquirer, 6

G

Garrison, William Lloyd, 12, 14, 22, 27
Grimke, Angelina and Sarah, 6

H

Howe, Julia Ward, 10
Howitt, William, 14
Hunt, Jane, 15

I

Iroquois, 15

M

M'Clintock, Mary Ann, 15
Miller, Alice Duer, 48
Mott, Lucretia, 7, 9, 12, 14, 15

N

National Women's Party, 44
National American Woman Suffrage Association (NAWSA), 10, 11, 39, 41-44, 48
National Woman Suffrage Association, 9, 10, 24, 27, 29, 39

O

O'Connell, Daniel, 14

P

Paul, Alice, 11, 44, 46, 48
Pillsbury, Parker, 29

R

Revolution, The, 9, 29

S

slavery, 6, 12-14, 17, 20, 22, 24, 27
Stanton, Elizabeth Cady, 7, 8, 9-10, 14-15, 20, 22, 24, 27, 29, 32, 37, 39, 41-44
Stone, Lucy, 9, 10, 20, 27

T

Truth, Sojourner, 8, 20

V

voting rights, 4, 9, 10, 11, 14, 15, 17, 20, 27, 29, 32-34, 37-50

W

Wilson, President Woodrow, 46, 48
"Woman's Bible, The," 10, 41-44
Women's Anti-Slavery Convention, 7
Women's New York Temperance Society, 8
Women's Political Union, 44
Woman's Rights Convention (Seneca Falls, NY), 7, 15, 17
Women's Suffrage Bill, 8
Wright, Frances, 6
Wright, Martha, 15

PRIMARY SOURCE LIST

Page 5: Letter from Abraham Lincoln to the *Sangamon Journal*, 1836. It is currently housed at the Library of Congress in Washington, D.C.

Page 13: Photograph of Lucretia Mott, circa 1870. It is currently housed at the Library of Congress in Washington, D.C.

Page 16: Photograph of the M'Clintock House. It is currently housed at the National Archives and Records Administration in College Park, Maryland.

Page 18: Advertisement for the First Woman's Rights Convention, 1848. It is currently housed at the Library of Congress in Washington, D.C.

Page 19: Declaration of Sentiments by Elizabeth Cady Stanton. It is currently housed at the Library of Congress in Washington, D.C.

Page 21: Text of Sojourner Truth's speech "Ain't I a Woman?"

Page 22: Portrait of Sojourner Truth, circa 1864. It is currently housed at the Library of Congress in Washington, D.C.

Page 23: Portion of the speech given by William Lloyd Garrison at the Woman's Rights Convention in 1853. It is currently housed at the Library of Congress in Washington, D.C.

Page 25: Photograph from sometime between 1890 and 1910 of a daguerreotype taken in 1856 of Elizabeth Cady Stanton and her daughter, Harriot. It is currently housed at the Library of Congress in Washington, D.C.

Page 26: Petition by Elizabeth Cady Stanton, Susan B. Anthony, and Lucy Stone, 1865. It is currently housed at the Center for Legislative Archives in Washington, D.C.

Page 28: "A Petition for Universal Suffrage," 1866. It is currently housed at the Center for Legislative Archives in Washington, D.C.

Pages 30-31: *The Revolution*, 1868. It is currently housed at the National Archives and Records Administration in College Park, Maryland.

Page 33: Cover of pamphlet of Carrie S. Burnham's argument for suffrage, 1873. It is currently housed at the Center for Legislative Archives in Washington, D.C.

Page 34: Account 1 of Susan B. Anthony's trial from the *Rochester Democrat and Chronicle*, 1873. It is currently housed at the Kansas Historical Society in Topeka, Kansas.

Page 36: Photograph of Susan B. Anthony from sometime between 1880 and 1906. It is currently housed at the Library of Congress in Washington, D.C.

Page 38: Text of speech by Susan B. Anthony titled "Social Purity," 1875.

Page 40: Portrait of Elizabeth Cady Stanton and Susan B. Anthony from sometime between 1880 and 1902. It is currently housed at the Library of Congress in Washington, D.C.

Page 42: Cover of the speech "Solitude of Self" by Elizabeth Cady Stanton, 1892. It is currently housed at the Library of Congress in Washington, D.C.

Page 43: Cover of the pamphlet titled "Bible and Church Degrade Women" by Elizabeth Cady Stanton, 1898. It is currently housed at the Center for Legislative Archives in Washington, D.C.

Page 45: Photo of the women's suffrage headquarters in Cleveland, Ohio, in 1912. It is currently housed at the Library of Congress in Washington, D.C.

Page 46: Cover of the program from the Woman Suffrage Procession held in Washington, D.C. on March 3, 1913. It is currently housed at the Library of Congress in Washington, D.C.

Page 47: 1917 map of states that won women's suffrage. It is currently housed at the National Archives and Records Administration in College Park, Maryland.

Page 49: Poem by Alice Duer Miller from a book titled *Are Women People?*, 1917. It is currently housed at the Library of Congress in Washington, D.C.

Page 50: Photo of women voting in New York City, 1917. It is currently housed at the Library of Congress in Washington, D.C.

About the Author
Colleen Adams is an editor and writer of children's books. She lives in Lockport, New York, with her husband and two children.

Photo Credits
Cover, p. 1 © Hulton/Archive/Getty Images; pp. 5, 13, 18, 19, 22, 23, 25, 33, 34, 36, 40, 43, 45, 46, 47, 49, 50 © Library of Congress; p. 16 © National Park Service Women's Right; pp. 26, 28, 30–31 © National Archives and Records Administration in College Park, Maryland; p. 42 © Cady Stanton Trust/Coline Jenkins-Sahlin.

Editor
Annie Sommers

Series Design
Nelson Sá